Words F

by
Ian Barclay

Glencairn

Published in 2015 by Glencairn

ISBN Paperback : 978-0-9933721-0-0

ISBN Ebook: 978-0-9933721-1-7

Published with the help of Indie Authors World

Photographs courtesy of Victoria Dixon & Jamie Campbell of the Foter community

About the Author

Ian Barclay became a registered celebrant with the Humanist Society Scotland in 2006. Under their auspices he has conducted numerous legal marriages, baby namings and funerals. The inspiration for this book comes from his practical experience in composing and conducting these ceremonies, allied to his lifelong love of writing poetry.

Acknowledgements

I would like to thank my wife Jean for her advice, support and endless patience throughout the writing of this book. I also wish to thank Sinclair and Kim Macleod of Indie Authors World for their invaluable assistance in the book's preparation and presentation.

Contents

Weddings

Poems, Readings & Sayings

Rhythm

If your two hearts beat as one you are tuned into the most beautiful rhythm that life has to offer.

Two Hearts That Beat As One

Today's about togetherness
And a love that runs so true;
It's about expressing your feelings
In vows unique to you.

It's about a bright new future
Built on dreams that will not fade;
It's stepping forth on a journey
And living the plans you've made.

Today's a celebration
Of a new life just begun;
Two minds that will grow together,
Two hearts that will beat as one.

Look At Us Now

I remember that first day
When you and I met;
A totally chance meeting,
One I'll never forget.
You filled all my senses
And captured my heart,
Turned my world upside down,
Gave my dreams a new start.

And look at us now,
Joined in body and mind,
Our lives merged together,
Our dreams intertwined.
On this day of all days
Everything feels so right;
Love is all around us
And our future is bright.

We stand on the threshold
Of a bold new life,
Avowed to each other
As husband and wife.
Together we are stronger
For true love empowers;
Let's both say, 'I do',
And the dream will be ours.

Precious Moments

The joy of togetherness is not only about exchanging kind words but in sharing those precious moments when there's no need to say anything at all.

Lucky Stars

Each day I thank my lucky stars
That you've come into my life,
To kiss away my darkest fears,
To soothe my struggles and strife;
And now you stand beside me
On this day you'll be my wife.

Each day I thank my lucky stars
For a love that's so sublime,
For its tenderness and sweetness,
For its harmony and rhyme.
Now it's time to tie the knot
To be united through all time.

Each day I thank my lucky stars
For everything you've done,
For your love and your caring,
For your beauty and your fun...
And here's the most amazing thing -
We have only just begun!

I Had A Dream

I had a dream that one day,
Just maybe one day,
I'd meet someone
A lot like you.

I had a dream that on that day,
When I met that certain someone,
Maybe, just maybe,
He would like me too.

I had a dream that in time,
Just maybe in time,
Our friendship would grow
Into a love so true.

Now, on our wedding day,
There are no maybes,
Just a joyous certainty
As we say, 'I do'.

A Haiku For Lovers

Love is a flower
That began as tiny shoots
And reached for the sun

Two Moving Forward As One

Marriage brings together two individuals whose hearts tell them they will only achieve their full potential by moving forward through life together as one. For them there are no doubts or uncertainties; just an unshakable belief that their unconditional love for each other will conquer all as they aspire to achieve everything their hearts desire.

Your Big Day

You've planned and prepared for over a year,
And now at last, your *Big Day* is here;
A day to celebrate with those close at heart,
A day filled with magic right from the start.

Your wedding party so proud and excited,
Your guests all smiling and truly delighted;
Music and poetry, promises and rings,
Are some of the joys this special day brings.

Champagne, formal photos, favours and fun,
Fine dining, cutting the cake; the party's begun.
Speeches and toasts and a special first dance,
An evening packed full of love and romance.

It's a day you'll treasure the rest of your life,
This first day together as husband and wife.
May the years bring joy in all that you do,
May your love stay strong, steadfast and true.

You Are My World

You are the sunshine in my smile,
The rainbow in my tears,
The gentle breeze that lifts me up,
The one who soothes my fears.

You are the stardust in my eyes,
The moon that lights my way,
The fire that burns in my heart,
The love of my life every day.

Riches

Life's greatest riches aren't to be found in a treasure chest, but in the hearts that beat in the chests of those who love you.

Someone So Rare

Today I marry someone so rare,
I'm told she's one in a million.
But to me she's much more special than that...
I'd say she's one in a trillion!

Today I marry the lady I love,
The one who has stolen my heart.
It's the day we become husband and wife,
And there's nothing can tear us apart.

Today I marry my beautiful bride,
Looking lovelier than ever before.
She's pledging to me her eternal love;
I couldn't ask for anything more.

Contentment

Contentment is snuggling up together on the sofa watching an old romantic movie… and falling blissfully asleep on each other's shoulder.

Love Is All

Those truly in love can find it all -
Honesty in the eyes that shine only for you
Trust in being able to share your deepest feelings
Reassurance in a hug that calms your insecurities
Hope in gazing at the stars and daring to dream
Comfort in a smile that melts your darkest mood
Delight in a kiss that makes your world brighter
Ecstasy in a touch that takes you to a higher plane
Caring in the hand that wipes your fevered brow
Fulfilment in knowing that your life has meaning
Beauty in sharing your life with the one you love

A Wonderful Journey

As a newly married couple you are about to embark upon a wonderful journey. Together there is nothing you can't achieve, no dream you can't fulfil. Be prepared, however, to encounter obstacles along the way. There may be rocky roads, steep inclines and diversions that will test your commitment and perseverance. But your love for each other will enable you to stay on the right track. On your married journey, it is not so much about burning up the road as in finding the love that burns within.

The Butterfly of Love

Love is like a butterfly
So precious and so rare;
It dances in the sunshine
Just like the love you share.

It lights up nature's garden
As it shimmers and it glows;
Bringing smiles to lovers' faces,
Spreading joy where ere it goes.

It flits from place to place
Then visits you one day,
When it's multi-coloured beauty
Will take your breath away.

But like that butterfly sublime
With its fragile satin wings,
Cherish the love you two have found
And the wonder that it brings.

When you stroll in the summer sun,
Pause to watch the butterflies play;
Be reminded of the love you share
And the vows you made this day.

Gloriously United

You come here as bride and groom
On this most special day in your life;
The day you begin a magical journey,
Joined together as husband and wife.

You'll reach for the stars together
And you'll find your place in the sun;
No longer as two individuals
But gloriously united as one.

With the planets all suitably aligned,
Everything's destined to work out right.
We wish you good luck on your journey;
May your love burn eternally bright.

Happiness

Happiness doesn't come from seeking a pot of gold at the end of the rainbow but in finding golden moments to share with the one you love.

Building A Strong Foundation

Marriage is the foundation upon which you can build a meaningful and lasting relationship. Its strength and endurance will come from your unconditional love for each other and your desire to be caring, trusting and supportive at all times. Go forth together and live out your marriage vows every day of your life… and be the best husband and wife you can be.

Kiss And Make Up

Never go to bed on an argument but always kiss and make up. Then you can wake up the next morning full of hope for the day ahead.

I Know I Am Where I Belong

When I wake up in the morning,
I feel your soft breath on my face
And I know I am alive.
I know I am where I belong.

When I have a break at my job,
I stare into my coffee cup
And see us slow-dancing.
I know I am where I belong.

When I return from work,
I feel your sweet lips on mine
And my heart skips a beat.
I know I am where I belong.

When I go to bed at night,
I feel your soft skin against mine
And I feel warm inside.
I know I am where I belong.

With You I Feel So Special

You make my eyes light up when you look at me
You make my heart flutter when you are near me
You make me breathless when you kiss my lips
You make me quiver when you whisper in my ear
You make me melt inside when you hold me tight
You make me feel so special

Your Marriage Vows

The marriage vows you make to each other on your wedding day are not just words - they are the bedrock upon which your marriage is built. Hold your vows dear and, as you go through life together, keep them forever at the forefront of your mind and etched into your heart. Only then will your marriage grow, develop and flourish into something truly beautiful and everlasting.

You Make My Life Complete

You support me without trying to control me
You get close to me without suffocating me
You laugh *with* me without laughing *at* me
You talk to me without talking down to me
You read my mind without speaking for me

You give me all you have without conditions
You bring so much sunshine into my world
You say 'I love you' and I know you mean it
You teach me the meaning of togetherness
You create a sense of belonging in my life

You let me share your hopes and dreams
You help me see the world more clearly
You lift me up when I stumble and fall
You believe in me as I believe in you
You walk with me everywhere I go

You bring out the best in me
You make my life complete

Sunshine

It may be raining, snowing or blowing a gale outside but, when you're in love, there will always be sunshine in your heart.

The Ring Of Life

On this day you are married your wedding ring will shine brightly; a band of gold signifying strength, wholeness and unity. As you go through married life, your ring will inevitably become scratched and dulled as life rubs up against it. Nevertheless, it will remain as precious to you as it is today; a symbol of eternal love and sharing, a talisman against life's ups and downs. Wear it with pride.

The One

When you share your life with the right person;
The one you love so deeply with all your heart,
The one you share your hopes and dreams with,
The one you laugh with and the one you cry with,
The one you are relaxed and totally at peace with,
The one you call your best friend and soul mate,
The one you choose to have children with;
Then you have found The One,
The one and only special one
To share your life's journey.

May You Find It All

May the pleasures you find be many
May the setbacks you encounter be few
May your bond of friendship never waver
May your love burn brightly and true
May you never find a river you can't cross
May you never find a mountain you can't climb
May you never take a path that leads nowhere
May you walk hand in hand through all time

Home

It is important to keep up with the housework but it is doubly important to work at making your house a home.

It's Easy to Love You

It's easy to love you on the day we are wed
But I'll still love you when you push me out the bed
When you spend too much and we go into the red
When you go in the huff over something I've said
When you drink too much wine and it goes to your head

It's easy to love you dressed in satin and lace
But I'll still love you with a mud pack on your face
When your hair's blowing around all over the place
When you can't park the car in a really big space
When without any reason you get on my case

It's easy to love you when we fool around and play
But I'll still love you when your hair's turning grey
When you ask me all too often, 'What did you say?'
When you take me out to dinner but I have to pay
When you know I'm right but you still have your way

It's easy to love you no matter what you do...
Because I'm truly and madly in love with you

I'll Show You

I'll show you how to wash the floor
How to buy goods from the store
How to work the washing machine
How to hang clothes on the green
How to polish and how to dust
How to be honest and how to trust
How to kiss away my fears
How to love me through the years
How to make me truly happy
How to change our baby's nappy...!

Changes

When a woman marries she gets to change her surname once… and change her mind as often as she likes!

Living The Dream

Life is for living,
Living is for loving,
Loving is for sharing;
And sharing your life
With the one you love
Is living the dream.

There's Nothing I Would Change

I don't always share your choice of T.V.
Or the types of music you play,
Or the places you go with some of your friends,
Or the things that fill up your day.
But there's nothing I would change or rearrange,
For I love you just as you are.
You are the world to me in every way;
My daybreak, my sunset, my star.

Togetherness

The success of a marriage isn't determined by the number of years you have spent together but by the togetherness you have found within those years.

Yesterday, Today & Tomorrow

Yesterday you were two individuals,
Today you are joined together as one,
Tomorrow you wake up as husband and wife.
How awesome is that!

You have travelled so far on your journey
But there is so much further you can go.
Together you have the world at your feet
And the possibilities are limitless.

Home

Home is a four letter word that can be defined as a four word phrase – a place to belong!

Marriage Vows

Examples Of Marriage Vows

(To be read from a card or repeated after your celebrant)

Option1

In the presence of our family and friends,

I give you my hand to hold, I give you my heart.

I promise to love and protect you,

support and encourage you;

be by your side through good times and bad;

bring laughter and sunshine into your life;

be your best friend and soul mate, for as long as we both shall live.

Examples Of Marriage Vows (continued)

Option2

In the presence of our family and friends,

I promise to love you completely as you love me;

trust you and be honest with you at all times;

support and share with you in all of life's decisions,

through triumph and uncertainty, laughter and tears,

for as long as we both shall live.

Option3

I promise to be the best husband/wife I can be;

love and cherish you unconditionally;

support and encourage you at all times,

for as long as we both shall live.

Choose Your Own Marriage Vows From This Selection

(To be read from a card or repeated after your celebrant)

In the presence of our family and friends...

With an open and trusting heart, and without hesitation, I join my life with yours.

I want to share in your dreams and I want you to share in mine.

You are my world and with you I am complete.

I give you my hand and give you my heart.

I pledge my life to you without conditions.

I promise to love and cherish you with all my heart.

I promise to love, honour and respect you through the varying circumstances of our life together.

I promise to love you unconditionally.

I promise to always be honest with you and to trust you completely.

I promise to be your best friend and soul mate.

I promise to bring laughter and sunshine into your life.

I promise to do all I can to make our home a happy one, filled with music, laughter and love.

I promise to respect your individuality and always try to understand any differences between us.

I promise to support and encourage you through joy and sadness, triumph and uncertainty, laughter and tears.

I promise to make you feel safe and secure.

I promise to be the best husband/wife I can be.

I promise to do all I can to make our life together a happy and fulfilling one.

I promise to learn from our shared experiences and build from them a full and loving marriage based on trust, respect and honesty.

I promise to respect and embrace your individuality.

I promise to give you a hug when you need one.

I promise to be by your side always, bringing you friendship, love, laughter and companionship.

I promise to live with you in a spirit of tolerance, trust and respect.

I promise to seek to live together as different yet equal individuals who recognise and accept each other's strengths and weaknesses.

I promise that whatever life may throw at us, I will do my best to guide us through it and help us move forward.

Choose Your Own Marriage Vows From This Selection (continued)

I promise to help create a secure home for our children.

I promise to stand firmly beside you as we build our future and work towards achieving our goals and realising our dreams.

I promise to foster a positive approach in all we do, so that we can grow and develop within our marriage to our mutual happiness and fulfilment.

I promise to offer help to you when you need it and not be afraid to ask for help when *I* need it.

I promise to be there for you and empathize with you through any difficult times.

...for as long as we both shall live.

Choose Your Own Marriage Vows From This Selection

(To be read out by your celebrant for you to reply 'I do')

Groom to Bride:

(Groom's name), in the presence of your family and friends, do you, without hesitation, join your life with *(Bride's name)*?

(I do)

As you give *(Bride)* your hand to hold, do you give her your heart, and do you promise to love and cherish her, support and encourage her, through good times and bad?

(I do)

Do you promise to bring laughter and sunshine into *(Bride)'s* life and be her best friend and soul mate for as long as you both shall live?

(I do)

(Groom), do you promise to love *(Bride)* unconditionally, trusting her completely and being honest with her at all times, while supporting and sharing with her through triumph and uncertainty, laughter and tears?

(I do)

Do you promise to be the best husband you can be to *(Bride)*, taking care of her the best you can, keeping her safe and comfortable, for as long as you both shall live?

(I do)

Choose Your Own Marriage Vows From This Selection (continued)

Do you promise to tell *(Bride)* every day that you love her, and do you promise to give her a hug when she needs one?

(I do)

***NB** Bride to Groom: as above with the roles/gender reversed.*

Choose Your Own Marriage Vows From This Selection

(To be read out for you to respond jointly, 'We will')

(Bride) and *(Groom),* in the presence of your family and friends, will you give your heart to each other and promise to love and cherish each other forever?

(We will)

Will you accept and embrace each other's individuality and try to understand any differences between you, and will you always be honest and trusting with each other?

(We will)

Will you bring laughter and sunshine into each other's lives, always be there for each other with encouragement and support, and be best friends and soul mates forever?

(We will)

Will you seek to have a loving marriage, allowing it and each other to change and develop while supporting each other through happiness and sorrow, health and illness?

(We will)

Will you seek to trust the ebb and flow of your love, accepting each other's strengths and weaknesses, and offer your love without conditions

(We will)

Choose Your Own Marriage Vows From This Selection (continued)

Will you seek to learn from your shared experiences and build from them a full and caring friendship based on love, trust and respect?

(We will)

Will you do all you can to be a brilliant husband and wife to each other, always giving a hug when needed?

(We will)

Consider Adding Your Own Personal Light-hearted Marriage Vows

(To be read from a card or repeated after your celebrant)

If you intend to inject light-heartedness into your otherwise serious vows, you may wish to consider writing something humorous that is personal to you as a couple... perhaps along the lines of the examples below.

<u>Groom:</u>

I promise to keep your feet warm in bed at night.

I promise to learn how to operate the washing machine.

I promise to keep calm when you spend too much at the sales.

I promise to get up during the night to investigate every strange noise you hear.

<u>Bride:</u>

I promise to use my cold feet to keep you cool in bed at night.

I promise to teach you to use the washing machine...and hang out the clothes.

I promise not to overspend unless I see a really good pair of shoes.

I promise not to panic when I hear a strange noise during the night.

Words For Your Celebrant To Introduce The Exchange Of Rings

Option1

(Bride) and *(Groom)* will now exchange rings as a symbol of the infinity and all-embracing perfection that is love.

Option2

The wedding ring is a circle; a symbol of wholeness, strength, co-operation and peace. The circle represents the seasons of life itself, a symbol of your love for each other through life's changing times.

Option3

These rings stand as a symbol of the love you share; the unbroken circle representing unending love, wholeness and peace. These rings are the permanent reminder of your love for one another and of the vows you exchange today.

Words For The Happy Couple To Say At The Exchange Of Rings

Option 1

(Name), I give you this ring as a symbol of my love for you. Please wear it always and, when we are apart, look upon it and think of me.

Option 2

(Name), I give you this ring shaped as a symbol of eternity. Please wear it as a sign of our love and as a reminder of the promises we have made today.

Option 3

(Name), as this ring surrounds your finger, so my love surrounds you, cherishing and protecting you always and forever.

Option 4

(Name), I place this ring around your finger as a symbol of my love for you, and the love that unites us today and forever.

Option 5

(Name), without hesitation and with an open and trusting heart, take this ring and with it my commitment to be the best husband/wife I can be.

Renewal Of Vows

(Husband's name) and *(Wife's name),* as you celebrate ** years of happily married life, you have chosen to formally reaffirm your love and commitment to each other by responding to the following questions posed as vows:

Will you continue to love and cherish each other; respect each other's individuality; show empathy in times of joy, uncertainty and sadness; trust and be honest with each other at all times?

(We will)

Will you continue to bring sunshine and laughter into each other's life; support and encourage each other in all of life's decisions; keep each other safe and secure; challenge routine with imagination and spontaneity?

(We will)

Will you continue to love and support your children (and grandchildren), sharing in their triumphs and good times, and helping them through any problems they may have?

(We will)

Will you continue to do everything you can to ensure the success you have achieved in your marriage to date is carried on into the future, and will you remain best friends and soul-mates for all time?

(We will)

Baby Namings

Poems, Readings & Sayings

Pride And Joy

As you journey through life you will have many outstanding moments, but none will come anywhere near the pride and joy you experience in bringing a child into this world.

We'll Always Be There

We'll always find time
For the smile in your eyes,
The glow on your face
With each new surprise.
We'll hold onto time,
For we know how it flies.

We'll always find time
To skip here and there,
Feel the warm summer sun,
And the wind in our hair.
We'll always find time,
We'll always be there.

Our Wish For You

Through life's bitter chills,
May you always be warm;
May you always find shelter
From the eye of the storm.

In Life's tangled forest,
May you find the right track,
And if you ever get lost
May you find your way back.

When you reach out for help,
May your loved ones deliver;
May the flame in your heart
Burn brightly forever.

The Power A Baby Possesses

Babies may be small and helpless but they possess strange, mystical powers. Adults who come in contact with them will inevitably fall under their spell, causing them to act out of character and talk funny. It will be as if they have become children again.

Baby Love

Your baby looks up at you
With those big, bright eyes
And that sweet, cute smile…
Then reaches out to you
And captures your heart.

From then until forever,
A unique bond is formed;
A bond that is unbreakable,
Unshakeable, unmistakeable;
A love beyond compare.

Go Forth My Little One

My dear and precious little one,
Believe what I say is true:
There's nothing in this whole wide world
You won't be able to do.

Of course you'll start with baby steps,
You'll stumble and you'll fall,
But soon you'll get the hang of things
And stride out walking tall.

So many things to see and do,
You won't know where to start,
But this advice I'd give to you -
Always follow your heart.

The world out there awaits you,
There's much to explore each day,
So go reach out and touch it...
We're behind you all the way.

Children Bring You So Much

Children introduce you to so many things. They take you places; places you would not have found without them. They encourage you to experience things; things you would not have experienced without them. They teach you things about yourself; things you would not have known without them. They bring so much richness into your life.

Simple Things

Being a parent isn't so much about doing great things for your child, but doing the simple things in a great way.

If I Could Paint A Dream

If I could paint my child a meadow,
It would be yellow, gold and green,
With tiny flecks of poppy red,
Like a Monet landscape I've seen.
You'd skip through wispy grasses
In your nonchalant, carefree way,
Singing so sweetly the song of life
From morning till end of the day.

If I could paint my child a sky,
It would be a hazy cobalt blue,
With tiny, fluffy, pure white clouds
And a sun shining brightly for you.
As the daylight begins to retreat,
I'd paint a sunset of orange red,
A night sky sparkling with stars,
And a moon smiling over your bed.

If I could paint my child a dream,
I'd paint a world without anger and greed;
A world that would always be kind to you,
And provide you with all that you need.
My dearest, sweetest, innocent child,
May your beauty always shine through;
May good health be with you forever;
May all of your dreams come true.

A Haiku For Parents

Mama and Dada
The most overwhelming words
A parent will hear

Spreading Sunshine

Children possess many gifts, not least of which is their ability to spread sunshine wherever they go.

Daddy's Girl

Daddy will bounce you on his knee
And throw you way up high,
He'll spin you around like an aeroplane
So you'll think that you can fly.

He'll take you to the local park,
The seaside, zoo and fair,
And any time you look around
Your Daddy will be there.

To him you'll always be special;
He'll be at your beck and call,
And always there to catch you
If ever you should fall.

You'll love your Daddy so much
And his love for you will be true;
If ever you land in a tight spot,
Your Daddy will know what to do.

He'll always be there to support you,
No matter what path you walk.
From now until his very last breath,
Your Daddy will be your rock.

Go for it

Go soar with the eagles
In mercurial flight;
Go fly to the sun
Burning so bright;
Go dance with the stars
In the clear winter night;
Go slide down the rainbow
In its shimmering light;
Go live out your dreams -
And just hold on tight!

Universe

When a loving couple move into a house it becomes a home. Add a child and it becomes the centre of their universe.

Being Small

Life's really tough
When you're small like me;
Wrapped up in a shawl
So I can't get free,
Strapped in a car seat
With nothing to see;
It isn't much fun,
I'm sure you'll agree.

Grown-ups talk funny
And throw me up high,
Bounce me on their knee,
Rock me when I cry.
They pass me around,
Goodness knows why;
Enough is enough,
And that is no lie!

But let's take a moment
To think all this through;
My parents read me stories,
Like Winnie the Pooh.
I've walkers and bouncers,
And cuddly toys too…
I'll stay small a bit longer -
Yes, that's what I'll do!

Spaceman

When I get a little older,
I'll journey to the stars;
In my silver rocket ship
I'll visit Venus and Mars.
I'll go to other planets,
A new one every day,
As I boldly travel onwards,
On through the Milky Way.

I'll visit a hundred planets
Before my mission's done;
I'll be master of the universe,
I'll be the number one.
It'll be fun being a spaceman,
The biggest thrill that I've had,
But I'll hurry back to earth …
For I'll miss my Mum and Dad!

The Greatest Investment Of All

The investment we make in our children is usually repaid many times over in the sheer delight we experience from sharing in their achievements and, ultimately, in watching them grow and develop into maturity. We hope they will become the best they can be and, in turn, pass on all their gathered knowledge and values to *their* children. It's the way of the world.

Precious

Tiny fingers and tiny toes,
Rosebud mouth and button nose,
Dainty pinks and frilly bows;
A little girl who loves to pose.

Big bright eyes, a toothless grin,
Downy hair and peach soft skin;
Wide awake or all tucked in,
She steals the hearts of doting kin.

Multi-coloured and never grey,
A ray of sunshine in every way.
Dearest (Baby's name), we have to say...
You become more precious every day.

Awesome

It's awesome that together you have created a life
It's awesome to hold your child in your arms
It's awesome to see your child smile back at you
It's awesome to feel your child's hand in yours
It's awesome to watch your child's first steps
It's awesome to hear the words *Mama* and *Dada*
It's awesome being a parent

The Team Behind You

I would say this to (*child's first name*): Your parents' love for you is unconditional and they will devote their lives to you. Your grandparents will form a special loving bond with you and there is so much you will learn from them. And, as children thrive in the widest possible community of love and affection, your circle of extended family and friends will also have a role to play in helping you find your place in the world. Everyone supporting you is part of a magical team - the *(child's full name)* team! They will be behind you all the way.

Imagination

Encourage your child's imagination to take flight, then jump on his magic carpet and let him take you on a journey to places lost in the mists of your childhood.

Character Building

(Winnie the Pooh style)

May you be imbued with the personality traits found in those endearing characters from Hundred Acre Wood, courtesy of A A Milne and Disney films.

May you have:

Pooh Bear's thoughtfulness and caring;
Christopher Robin's wisdom and maturity;
Tigger's energy and resourcefulness;
Kanga's kind-heartedness and patience;
Roo's curiosity and innocent sense of wonder;
Rabbit's leadership qualities;
Eeyore's caution;
Owl's friendliness;
Piglet's bravery.

May you lead a happy and fulfilling life.

My Little Brother

There's a very special boy,
Who I love more than any other;
His name is ***, he's ** months/years old;
He's my very own little brother.

When we get a little older,
I'll watch out for him at school.
It's great fun to be a big sister,
My little brother sure is cool.

When *** becomes a man,
Some people will call him Mister,
But even if he ends up taller than me…
I'll still always be his big sister!

I Love My Little Sister

I love my little sister so much
I love her smile, I love her touch
I love her fingers and her toes
I love her little button nose
I love her eyes that shine so bright
I love her squeezing my finger tight
I love her watching while I play
I love her more with every day

Achievement

It's important for a child to be aware that being successful is not always about coming first, but in challenging yourself to be all you can be. If you can achieve something today you couldn't achieve yesterday, you are a winner.

Naming Promises

Naming Promises From Parents

(To be read from a card or repeated after celebrant)

Father or Mother (on behalf of both):

In the presence of our family and friends,

I confirm that the name we have chosen for our beautiful daughter is *** (**) ***.

We promise to nurture and protect her,

love and support her, cherish and guide her,

respect her individuality,

and share in her triumphs and uncertainties.

We promise to show her how to respect others and the world around her,

teach her tolerance and understanding,

and always be there for her.

Nb. *Son/Him/His* can be substituted for *Daughter/Her.*

Naming Promises From Parents

(To be read out by your celebrant for you to reply 'Yes')

(Mother's name) and *(Father's name)*, in the presence of your family and friends, can you confirm that the name you have chosen for your beautiful daughter is *** (***) ****?

(Yes, it is.)

Do you promise to nurture and protect her; love and support her; cherish and guide her; respect her individuality; and share in her triumphs and uncertainties?

(Yes, we do.)

Will you show her how to respect others and the world around her; teach her tolerance and understanding; and always be there for her?

(Yes, we will.)

(Mother) and (Father), can you confirm it is *** ***** and *** ***** (plus any others) whom you have chosen to act as guardians to ***(child)?

(Yes, it is.)

Nb. *Son/Him/His can be substituted for Daughter/Her.*

Naming Promises From Guardians

(To be read out by celebrant for the guardians to collectively reply, 'Yes')

(1st Guardian's name) and *(Any other Guardian's name(s))*, in the presence of everyone here, do you confirm your commitment to act as guardians to *(child's name)*?

(Yes, we do.)

Will you always welcome *(Child)* if she comes to you for company, advice or help, and will you listen to her and respect her confidences no matter how great or small?

(Yes, we will.)

Further to this, will you show *(Child)* love and understanding, and will you let her know that she will always have a special place in your hearts?

(Yes, we will.)

---

*(***'s)* name having been officially pronounced and the promises and declarations of parents and guardians duly stated, I have great pleasure in saying –

It's a privilege to know you… (Child's full name)

Nb. *He/Him* can be substituted for *She/Her.*

Guardians can be titled Supporting Adults, Mentors, etc.

Funerals

Poems, Readings & Sayings

Special People

We all have to face the end and, as it nears, we can find comfort and peace in the knowledge that we didn't walk through this awesome world alone, but shared it with some very special people.

Just Let Me Be

Do not grieve, just let me be,
Death was quick and kind to me.
I felt no pain, I knew no fear,
Just calm acceptance the end was near.
No hanging around after the fact,
I left this world with dignity intact.

My journey of life is over and done,
For me, it was a wondrous one.
I've no regrets, I've savoured much;
Good friends, good times, a loved one's touch.
So be not burdened with tears of sorrow,
Treasure the past, but live for tomorrow.

Memories

As we enter our twilight years,
We are faced with a stark reality -
So much of our life lies behind us
And so little remains.
Time is so fleeting, so unforgiving;
It does no deals.

If we have used time well,
We can look back with a warm smile
And a happy heart.
Our memories will burn like embers,
To warm our creaking bones
And melt away our fears.

There will be assets to contemplate
And liabilities to evaluate.
In the final analysis, however,
The true measure of our worth
Is in the memories we leave etched
In the hearts of others.

Your Contribution

You enter this world with the love of your parents and, if you can leave it with the love of your children, you will have made a valuable contribution to humanity.

Something You Must Know

The light that shone upon me,
Is pale and flickering now.
The years lie long behind me,
Ahead, my final bow.

You ask if I've any regrets?
I'd say there's only one -
The pain I'll leave behind me,
When my life is done.

My dear and precious loved ones,
There is something you must know:
I've lived a life so rich and full...
And it's you who made it so.

Golden

Golden was the colour of your hair,
Your sweet, sweet smile
And your warm, unselfish heart.
It was the colour of your ring
With the diamonds that sparkled
In your eyes and in our dreams.

Golden was the colour of the fields
We strolled through in summertime,
And the colour of the blazing sun
That melted our fears
And filled our years.
Golden are the memories you left me.

Forget Me Not

Memories of you fill my senses like a profusion of forget-me-nots.

Walk On

When someone you love dies,
Your world crashes to a halt
And a cold, darkness descends.
You are lost in time and space
And there seems no way back.

You must summon up the strength
To confront and conquer the pain,
Come to terms with your loss,
And find a way out of the mire
Of your anguish and despair.

Realise your life was touched
By a truly wonderful person,
And be grateful for all you shared.
Find the courage to stand up
And walk on through the storm.

Words

I looked and you were gone,
No time to wonder why;
I didn't even get the chance
To say my last goodbye.
So many things were left unsaid
As shyness ruled my mood,
And I didn't say 'I love you'
Near as often as I should.

If only I could have you back,
Even for a moment or two,
For now I know the special words
That I would say to you:
You were my harbour in stormy seas,
The beacon that lit up my way,
The fire that burned in my heart,
The love of my life every day.

There's a dark cloud over my world;
I can't imagine life without you,
But somehow I need to go on,
For that's what you'd want me to do.
So I'll live life the best that I can,
Find my smile and try not to be sad;
I'll cherish the love that fills my heart
And be grateful for all that we had.

Quality Of Life

To have led a full life is nothing to do with the number of years you have lived and everything to do with the quality of life you put into each day you had.

Gone But Always There

She closed her eyes...
And melted into the soft velvet darkness,
Free now from the vagaries of this world;
Granted peace in a calm and timeless place,
A place befitting her grace and dignity.

No longer will she walk amongst us,
Spreading sunshine through our lives;
Ever generous with her love and support,
Her wisdom and calm reassurance,
Her gentle smile and warm embrace.

She nurtured us and loved us with all her heart,
Unselfishly putting us first at all times;
Spreading rose petals before us by day,
Sprinkling stardust as the night fell upon us;
Transferring her energy and goodness to us.

Her vision and imagination inspired us,
Her caring and understanding lives on within us.
She was our mother, our teacher, our best friend.
We don't fear life without her for she is not gone,
She lives on in our hearts and always will.

My Hero

My Grandpa is my hero,
He was such a special man;
There was nothing I liked better
Than to visit him and Gran.
We'd play games on the table
And wrestle on the floor.
I'd help him out with little jobs
And then we'd play some more.

My Grandpa is my hero,
I loved his big, warm smile;
He took me to the park some days
And we'd play there for a while.
He often took me into town
And always bought me sweets,
He also bought me books and toys
And lots of other treats.

My Grandpa is my hero,
He was simply always there
To answer all my questions,
To smile and ruffle my hair.
I'm sad that he is gone,
But I'm trying not to cry,
For Grandpa always told me
That heroes never die.

Friends

On your travels through life what matters is not so much the number of places you visited, but the number of friends you made along the way.

The Big Armchair

The big armchair is tired and worn,
But he wouldn't hear of replacing it.
They had gown old together
And he was the first to go.
Now I couldn't bear to part with it.

That chair suited him so well,
And he was such a presence in it.
A man amongst men; my man.
A strong yet kind and gentle man.
All the man I ever wanted.

His life is woven into the fabric of the chair
So that his essence still fills my senses.
I hear the echoes of children's laughter,
The whisper of his reassuring wisdom,
The rustle of his daily newspaper.

The big armchair glows in the firelight
And we are together again in the stillness.
I share with him my day and my feelings.
No one ever sits in the big armchair;
No one could ever take his place.

You

You came into my world
You stood there by my side
You kissed away my darkest fears
You gave me hope and pride

You placed your hand in my hand
You walked with me each mile
You sang to me the song of life
You made it all worthwhile

No Need To Fear Death

We have no need to fear death when we know that the essence of our being will live on in the hearts and minds of our children for generations to come.

Time

Time is a strange conundrum.
When we are young...
We have so much time,
But so little knowledge
Of how best to use it.

In our middle years...
We have knowledge and experience
And a measure of financial security,
But find the hands of time
Spinning round so fast.

In our latter years...
We have wisdom and understanding,
But our senses begin to fail us.
This is when time hangs heaviest
On our pleading heart.

Time is our monster and our master:
Unfathomable and unforgiving,
Mischievous and malevolent.
We must confront it yet respect it,
And hope we get the balance right.

A Haiku For A Funeral

We honour a life
That meant much to so many
And smile through our tears

Life Imitating Art

Life is like a painting, with you as the artist. You start with a blank canvas, applying texture and colour, but never quite sure how it will turn out in the end. You develop your own style, building upon your own experiences. You may be cautious and disciplined or you may be bold and expressive. Either way, you will make mistakes as you go. If you are wise, you will accept these as the nature of things and deal with them as best you can, stay focused and push on towards your goal. Eventually, your painting – your life – will have reached its conclusion and there will be no more to be done. The result will be something unique to you; something you can be proud of; something to be appreciated by others for countless years to come.

Missing You

I miss your soft, beguiling smile
I miss your laid back, easy style
I miss your hand in mine each mile

I miss your warm and sparkling eyes
I miss that look with each surprise
I miss your words so warm and wise

I miss the meals we shared at night
I miss the way you held me tight
I miss your bright and shining light

I miss your love that was so rare
I miss the things we used to share
I miss that you were always there

Remembered With A Smile

He may have had his worries,
But you'd never see him blue;
He always seemed contented
As he walked a path so true.

Nothing ever ruffled him,
You'd never hear him whine,
And if you asked him how he was,
He'd simply say, 'I'm fine!'

Perhaps a little old fashioned,
Somewhat set in his ways,
But always such a gentleman
Throughout his living days.

Always there when needed,
Our rock in every way.
We think of him so fondly,
On this most sombre day.

But he wouldn't want our tears,
For that was not his style,
So as we think of him today,
Let's do it with a smile.

Love Immortal

Love doesn't end with the death of a partner, for the remaining partner will carry forward that love for as long as he/she lives.

So Little Time

So little time...
To gaze in your eyes,
Feel your soft, tiny hand,
Express our goodbyes.
So little time,
How quickly it flies.

So little time...
To dance in the sun,
Go exploring your world,
Run free and have fun.
So little time,
A life barely begun.

So little time...
When a love runs so deep;
Questions without answers,
Stolen dreams, shattered sleep.
Yet so many fond memories,
A lifetime to keep.

True Love Never Dies

We lived within your daydreams,
We lived within your sleep,
We shared so much together
With a love that ran so deep.
Memories sweet and tender,
Forever ours to keep.

Memories of your smile,
Your bright, sparkling eyes,
The glow on your face
With each new surprise.
Your light shines forever,
True love never dies.

The Human Race

The great human race is a series of relays in which each of us will play our part. Whether yours is a sprint, a middle distance or a marathon, the joy is that you are able to take part. If you have given it your all and run a good race, you will justifiably feel proud. As you cross the finishing line, your senses will be filled with all the magical moments of your race. And it will be that feeling you take with you into the golden afterglow. Those who have supported you will be sad that your race is over but they will want to celebrate it and tell others about it. Memories of you and the race you have run will be etched in their hearts and minds for all time, inspiring them to make the most of *their* race. In the great human race, whatever distance you run, your contribution can only ever be relatively small… but you can make a huge difference to those around you!

Value Of Your Life

The real value of your life is not measured by the number of happy moments you experienced, but by the number of people who were sad when you passed away.

Words For A Committal

Commital At A Crematorium

Will you please stand.

In affection and respect, we have been remembering the life of *** (***) ****. Here in this last act, in sorrow but with love and appreciation, we bid him farewell.

Every living being has a beginning and an end.

For each of us there is a time to be born and a time to die.

So death has come to *** and now, as we bid him farewell, we commit his character and personality to our memories, and his love and friendship to our hearts.

We commit his body to its final end, to rejoin the great cycle of nature of which we are all a part.

- Curtains Close -

Will you please be seated.

NB. *Her* can be substituted for *Him/His*.

Commital At A Cemetry

I know that ***'s character and personality will be forever in your minds and her love and friendship forever in your hearts.

Here, in this last act, we commit the body of *** (***) **** to its natural end, to the earth which sustained and nourished her for so many years and which regenerates all life.

*** will be a part of this place for all time. Through the warmth of summer and the cold of winter, through the freshness of spring and the mists of autumn, she will be at peace.

NB. *His/He can be substituted for Her/She*

Lightning Source UK Ltd.
Milton Keynes UK
UKOW06f0121261015

261391UK00001B/2/P

9 780993 372100